HOW TO make a BETTER WORLD

Written by Keilly Swift
Illustrated by Rhys Jefferys

Foreword by Jamie Margolin

Can I really change the world?

Every one of us has the ability to make a change. Yes, the world is a very big place, and we can't control a lot of what happens in it. But if you start small, it is possible that one day your changes could influence a lot of people. For now, just remember that whoever you are, wherever you are, there's a way to make a change that is the right size for you.

Earth

We all know that the Earth needs our help, whether it's protecting animals or preventing pollution. Learn how to defend the Earth in **Chapter 4: Environment**

Activists use leaflets and posters to spread their message.

Humanity

Working for more fairness for everyone is one of the most amazing things a person can do. Become an amazing activist by reading **Chapter 3: Humanity**

Marches are a powerful way to protest.

Society

Society is made up of all the people living in the world. What our society is like is decided by how everyone chooses to behave. We each have a responsibility to make our society a kind, supportive, and safe place to be.

Conservation

Animals need to be protected from threats such as habitat loss and climate change. Helping animals survive is called wildlife conservation.

Being an activist means using your voice.

You

Before you help others, you often need to help yourself. Try some self-care tips to strengthen your mind and body in **Chapter 1: You**

Your journey to making the world a better place starts at home, with your family.

Teachers can help you with projects at school.

Community

Everyone needs to feel like they belong. Work to make your school, neighborhood, or town a better place to be in **Chapter 2: Community**

Contents

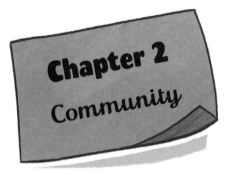

Chapter 2
Community

Chapter 1
You

 Penguin Random House

Author Keilly Swift
Illustrator Rhys Jefferys
Educational consultant Jenny Lane-Smith
Senior Editor Satu Hämeenaho-Fox
Senior Art Editor Fiona Macdonald
Project Art Editor Emma Hobson
Editorial Assistant Katie Lawrence
US Senior Editor Shannon Beatty
US Editor Margaret Parrish

Producer, Pre-Production Sophie Chatellier
Producer John Casey
Jacket Coordinator Issy Walsh
Jacket Designer Elle Ward
Senior Picture Researcher Sumedha Chopra
Managing Editors Laura Gilbert, Jonathan Melmoth
Managing Art Editor Diane Peyton Jones
Senior DTP Designer Neeraj Bhatia
Creative Director Helen Senior
Publishing Director Sarah Larter

First American Edition, 2020
Published in the United States by DK Publishing
1450 Broadway, Suite 801, New York,
New York 10018

Text copyright © Keilly Swift 2020
Foreword text copyright © Jamie Margolin 2020
Copyright in the layouts and design of the Work
shall be vested in the Publisher.
DK, a Division of Penguin Random House LLC
20 21 22 23 24 10 9 8 7 6 5 4 3 2 1
001–316625–March/2020

Chapter 3
Humanity

Chapter 4
Environment

A catalog record for this book is available from the Library of Congress.
ISBN 978–1–4654–9087–2

DK books are available at special discounts when purchased in bulk for sales promotions, premiums, fund-raising, or educational use. For details, contact: DK Publishing Special Markets, 1450 Broadway, Suite 801, New York, New York 10018 SpecialSales@dk.com

Printed and bound in China

A WORLD OF IDEAS:
SEE ALL THERE IS TO KNOW

www.dk.com

Young people have more power
to create change than we know.

I used to think I was too young to change
the world. But a series of events unfolded while
I was still in high school that led me to start an
international movement called Zero Hour.
Now, it organizes large student mobilizations
for climate action all over the world.

I learned by doing it myself. I am a kid who does not
come from any fame, wealth, or power, but I discovered
that I could make a big impact anyway—which
means so can YOU.

In this book, you will find the inspiration you need
to get your change-making journey started.

Welcome to the youth activist family!

Jamie Margolin

Feeling good, believing in yourself, and taking care of your mind and body are really important. Making a positive difference in the world starts by looking after yourself and those around you. This chapter looks at how the power to make a better world begins inside YOU!

World peace
I want to live in a peaceful world where there is no war or violence.

Equality for all
My wish is for everyone to be treated fairly regardless of race, religion, gender, age, or physical ability.

Animal welfare
My hope is that we can protect animals and make sure that no more species become extinct.

Share your wish for the future...

What do you wish for?

If you could grant a wish for the world, what would it be? We can't wave a magic wand, but we can all work toward a better world. Just use your imagination...

Freedom of speech

I wish for a world where everyone can speak up for what they believe in.

Clean oceans

I hope that one day the world's oceans will be plastic-free, so sea creatures can live safely and freely.

Planet safety

I'd love to live in a world where everyone takes responsibility for keeping our beautiful fields, woods, streets, rivers, and beaches clean.

Better lives for kids

My hope is that our future is bright and full of exciting opportunities and possibilities for all young people.

Kindness revolution

I'd like everyone to look out for each other so that no one feels isolated or excluded.

Fill up on healthy foods!

Keep your body running well by aiming for seven servings of different-colored fruits and vegetables every day. Don't worry if you have the occasional day that's less healthy— everyone does! It's what you do most of the time that matters.

Make a smoothie or add fruit to any dessert.

Snack on berries

Practice mindfulness

Focusing on what you can see, hear, smell, or taste in the present moment promotes calmness and well-being.

Relax your muscles from head to toe.

Take a deep breath

Self-care

Before you can help others, you need to make sure you're looking after yourself. Try some self-care tips to strengthen your mind and body.

Walk or cycle to school

Cycling is better for the environment than driving—and it's good exercise.

Get active

Exercise strengthens your body, gives you energy, and makes you feel great! The trick is to find an activity you enjoy, whether it's playing on the soccer team, swimming laps, or walking with your family.

Listen to calming music

Sleep well

Getting enough quality sleep is vital for good health. Kids need around 10 hours every night. Having a regular bedtime and winding down before you sleep can help ensure that you catch enough Zzzzzzs.

Avoid screens for at least an hour before bed.

Stroke a pet's fur

Kindness

The smallest kind deed can have a bigger effect than you realize. Being kind lifts everyone up and, in turn, creates more kindness.

Kindness jar

With your family or school class, fill a jar with lots of suggestions for kind things to do. Whenever you want to create some kindness, pick a note out of the jar.

Tell a friend a thing you like about them.

Write a silly rhyme to make people laugh.

Surprise a family member with a handmade gift.

The power of invitations

Try to make sure no one's left out of a gathering or group, especially if they're new to your class or area. It's always nice to know you're welcome... and inviting others usually means you'll get lots of invitations in return!

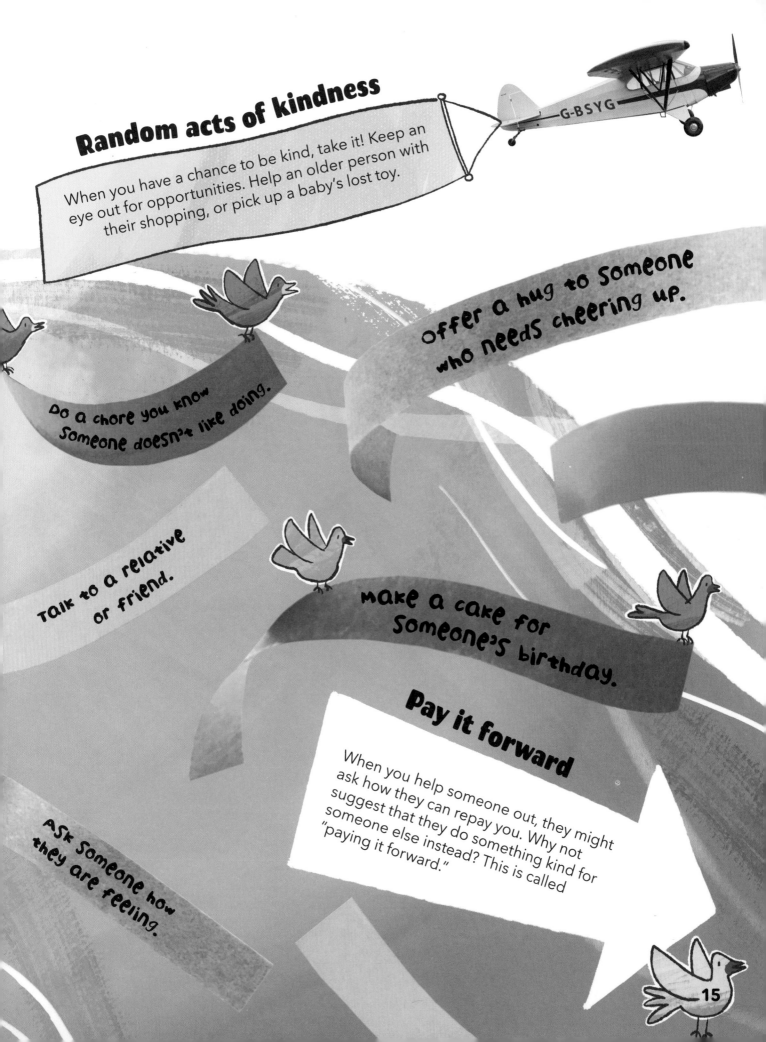

Random acts of kindness

When you have a chance to be kind, take it! Keep an eye out for opportunities. Help an older person with their shopping, or pick up a baby's lost toy.

Offer a hug to someone who needs cheering up.

Do a chore you know someone doesn't like doing.

Talk to a relative or friend.

make a cake for someone's birthday.

Pay it forward

When you help someone out, they might ask how they can repay you. Why not suggest that they do something kind for someone else instead? This is called "paying it forward."

Ask someone how they are feeling.

15

Feeling life's ups and downs

Happy
Happiness can range from contentment to joy. What makes you happy?

Surprised
If something happens unexpectedly (good or bad), your body tenses in preparation for action.

Excited
When anticipating something fun, you might feel jittery and your heart might beat fast.

Angry
Anger can make you feel hot and shaky. It can make you want to shout or cry.

Emotions are like a roller coaster... they go from high to low or do a loop!

Noticing the strength of your emotions can be helpful.

During the course of each day, you will probably feel a whole range of emotions. Learning to recognize your feelings is a useful skill. What emotions have you felt today?

Scared

Fear can make your breathing and heart rate faster. You might tremble or sweat more.

Sad

Sad feelings can be overwhelming. They might come with tears, a tight chest, or "a lump in your throat."

Embarrassed

When you feel ashamed, you might look down and your face may get red and feel hot.

Disgusted

Disgust is often described as a sick feeling deep in your stomach.

Proud

Hold your head high! It feels great to achieve something you set out to do.

Sometimes you feel many emotions at once.

Give a name to each emotion, even if it's mild.

Emotions can get stronger depending on the situation.

Intense emotions can sometimes feel overwhelming.

Strength of emotion

Figure out how strongly you feel an emotion by rating it on a scale of 1 to 10. Strong emotions can be hard to handle, but it's okay to feel them.

1   2   3   4   5   6   7   8   9   10

Waves of emotion

Powerful emotions can feel like waves crashing over you. They often come with physical sensations, such as a fluttery stomach or a tight chest. Finding the right strategies can help you ride the waves.

Channeling emotions

Here are some of the ways you can give powerful feelings an outlet. Try a few different techniques to learn what works best for you.

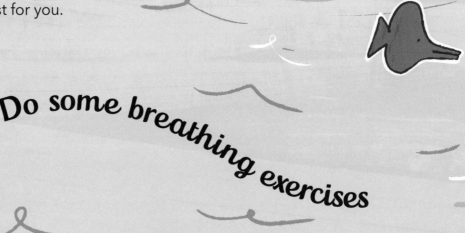

Do some breathing exercises

Focus your emotions on an art project

Express yourself in writing

Sailing through the storm

When you're having a tough time, you can feel isolated. It can often help to connect with people who have had similar experiences.

Go out for a run

Talk to someone you trust

Listen to music

Getting help

If you are struggling emotionally, speak to a trusted adult about whether you would benefit from seeing a counselor.

I stand up for what I believe in.

I can do anything I put my mind to.

When you have doubts, give yourself a pep talk.

I have courage and confidence.

Repeat phrases that boost your self-esteem.

Choose phrases that are personal to you.

The power of

I will face my fears.

I can change things for the better.

Believing you have the power to do something makes all the difference.

Sometimes a goal seems too big or far away for you to tackle. Being positive makes a goal more likely to happen. Train your brain by repeating a positive phrase, known as an affirmation.

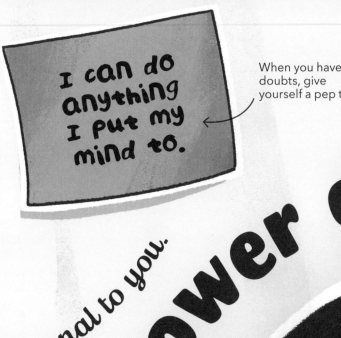

A mood board of me!

A mood board is a collection of pictures, words, and ideas with a theme. Put together one that reflects the different parts of you.

Get artsy

Whether you use a bulletin board or stick your items into a scrapbook, you can get as creative as you like with your mood-board display.

Your creativity

Add pictures of things you've created that make you proud. They could be poems, artwork, costumes, or crazy cakes!

Your pets and other favorite animals

Add photos of beloved pets, your top five animals, or cute critters doing funny things!

Your hobbies

Capture the ways you spend your free time, whether it's doing yoga, playing for a team, or being in a book club.

Important people in your life

Remind yourself of the people you care about with photos of parents, grandparents, and siblings (even if they annoy you sometimes!).

People you admire

Are you a fan of a particular singer, band, author, activist, or sportsperson? Add a photo of them in action, or write out one of their quotes in gorgeous handwriting.

A letter to future me!

Have you ever thought about what you might be like in the future? Picture yourself in five or 10 years' time and try writing yourself a letter. Write about you and your life now, the things you've learned, what you hope for, and any advice you have for future you.

Agreeing to disagree

When you feel strongly about a topic, it can be hard to hear that someone disagrees with you. It's important, however, to consider things from other points of view, even if you don't end up changing your mind.

Listen

Pay attention to what the person is saying and don't talk over them or rush in with your view. Repeat their key points to show you were listening to what they said.

Say how you feel

When you respond, try saying things like, "That's an interesting view, but here's why I disagree...." If they try to interrupt, politely ask if they will let you finish.

Show respect

Don't put the other person down or dismiss their views with negative comments. Try to understand the reasons for the way they feel. Particular experiences they've had may influence their viewpoints.

Don't get personal

Remember, it's just that one point of view you disagree with. Don't get angry with the other person and never resort to insults.

Stay calm

It can be a challenge to stay calm when you feel passionately about something. Take time out if you feel the discussion is getting heated!

It's not about winning or losing

You don't have to end up agreeing. It's hearing each other out and respecting each other's opinions that leads to a kinder, more understanding world.

Communities happen when people gather together. They can be built around the school you attend, the place you live, or something special you have in common with others. In this chapter, you'll discover ways you can make the world better through amazing communities.

What is a community?

A community is a group you belong to, from the wider community you live in to smaller groups that have things in common.

After-school club

It's great to find a community of friends that shares your interests. An after-school club is a fun way to share a hobby, whether it's drawing or a sport.

Cleanup Saturday

Everyone who lives in your area is part of the same community. See if you can join community activities, such as litter collection, to keep the area you live in clean and pleasant.

Young caregivers club

Life can throw unexpected challenges at you. For example, young people who care for a relative often feel lonely and stressed out. Support groups for people going through the same things can help.

Befriending

Making friends across generations helps create strong communities.

Shared history

Sharing and exploring your culture (and faith, if you have one) is an important type of community for many people. Some people gather at places of worship, while others make sure to keep family traditions going in the home.

Dare to be different

We can't all fit in all of the time. Maybe you're the only person you know who likes coin collecting, old music, or quirky fashion. Start a club and you might find others who think they're the only one of their kind, too!

Games club

You can start a new community with a shared activity. Organize a chess tournament or a friendly Snakes and Ladders club.

How to be a **great friend**

Strong friendships help us through the bad times and make the good ones even better. Here's a guide to the many ways that friends can be there for each other.

Help friends feel **appreciated**

Take time to say thank you. Send a handwritten note, give a call, or say thanks in person.

Buddy McFriend
21 Amigo Road
Paltown

Make people feel **included**

It's nice to be part of a group, but check that no one's feeling left out or ganged up on. You'll make a bond with someone who will then be sure to look out for you, too.

Respect your friends' **differences**

Celebrate the things that make your friends unique and special, from their culture and heritage to their hobbies and interests.

A tricky job takes far less time when it's shared. Then there's more time for playing.

Lend a hand when you can

Whether it's talking through a problem or just taking someone's mind off difficulties by having fun, good friends are there when times are tough.

Support and listen to each other

Friendship fallouts

Even the best of friends have times they don't get along perfectly. If that happens, use these tips to get your friendship back on track. You might find it becomes stronger than ever.

Discuss your feelings with a grown-up for a different view.

Talk it through.

Be **forgiving** and don't hold a grudge.

Be prepared to say **sorry**.

Try to **understand** why they, or you, have behaved in a certain way.

Yokohama, Japan, present day

The story of a place

What's the hidden history of where you live? Perhaps it has a surprising past or is the site of an unsolved mystery. Your local librarian can help you find out.

Canals of Yokohama, Japan, 1922

Celebrating heritage

Heritage is something that's passed down through generations, in families and communities. People share and celebrate their heritage through old traditions and shared memories.

It's a tradition

Traditions, such as the special days you celebrate, often come from your family's culture or faith. Your family may also have some unique traditions and rituals that they invented!

Mexican Day-of-the-Dead sugar skull

Food, glorious food

When you eat special food for a celebration or cook up an old family recipe, try imagining your ancestors enjoying the same feast.

Coffee cake

Family recipe

Sound of history

From Spanish flamenco guitar to Japanese taiko drumming, a country's heritage lives on through its music and songs.

Unlocking history

Ask older relatives about their history—they may be able to show you their photos. The past often holds dramatic stories, from love stories to journeys across the world.

Women's March 2017

When lots of people come together, they can make a big splash. This is what happened in the 2017 Women's March, the biggest protest ever seen in the US.

One action...

...leads to another

Politicians

Elected officials, such as congresswoman Alexandria Ocasio-Cortez, make choices on behalf of the people who live in the area they represent. A letter from you could influence their opinion.

If you are new to activism, try something small like writing a letter to a local official. You might persuade them to take action on air pollution or books for schools.

One small step

Every big movement started somewhere. A small step could inspire someone else to make a change. Who knows where that person will take your message?

"You are never too small to make a

Parkland students

Inspired by the Women's March, students at Marjory Stoneman Douglas High School in Florida organized a huge protest against gun violence.

Greta's sit-in

In 2018, Swedish teenager Greta Thunberg heard about what the Marjory Stoneman Douglas students had done. She started protesting to draw attention to climate change.

Climate strike

Following Greta's lead, more than a million children across the world joined climate strikes on September 20, 2019.

Others may join you...

...to fight for change

#trending

Social media can be a powerful tool. You could ask a trusted adult to host an account for you.

Every great person in a history book had to start somewhere. You never know where your small steps will take you!

difference." —Greta Thunberg

Volunteering

A beach or park cleanup has huge benefits for you and your community. It's an easy way to get dramatic results and it's also a fun day out. See if there's a cleanup going on near you, or ask an adult to help you organize one.

Litterbugs
Every piece of litter dropped is adding to the pollution problem.

Plastic problems
Litter not only looks bad, but it's also a danger to wildlife. Animals can choke on or get tangled in pieces of plastic.

Join a beach cleanup

The problem of beach litter becomes easier to tackle when lots of volunteers come together at cleanup events. The difference the effort can make is staggering!

Good times

Volunteering is a good way to get active, be outside, and make new friends. It is proven to make people feel happier.

Avoid hazards on a beach cleanup by following the organizer's safety advice.

Put a stop to bullying

What is bullying?

Bullying is behavior intended to hurt someone physically or emotionally. It may be aimed at a person because of their race, religion, gender, background, disability, or other difference.

Cyber

Cyberbullying is when someone sends insults, makes threats, or bothers others online. It can be anonymous, which means you can't tell who is sending the messages.

Physical

Bullying can take the form of physical hurt, including hitting or kicking, tripping someone, or stealing their belongings.

If you are the one being bullied, you are not alone.

Create a circle of trust

Bullying can make someone feel lonely, anxious, and sad. Offering friendship and listening to them can make all the difference.

It's sometimes easy to get swept along with a group, but try to make sure no one ever feels bullied. You won't regret doing the right thing.

Bullying affects many people and has a big impact on their mental health. It can feel impossible to escape from bullying, but it can be done if we work together.

39

Stand up to bullying

It's important not to ignore bullying, but you should never put yourself in danger. The most powerful thing you can do is to speak up and report bullying to an adult.

Verbal

Bullying can be done with words, which can range from teasing and name-calling to making threats.

It's okay to share your feelings about bullying.

Social

This type of bullying includes spreading rumors about someone or leaving them out of a group.

Never okay

There are often reasons for bullying behavior. Someone might be lashing out because they have a difficult home life, or they have been bullied themselves. Regardless, bullying should always be stopped.

Inspiring young people

A right to education

"One child, one teacher, one pen, and one book can change the world. Education is the only solution." Malala, addressing the UN Youth Assembly, 2013.

Greta Thunberg

Swedish climate activist Greta Thunberg has inspired school climate strikes across the world. She says having Asperger's helps her to think differently.

Malala Yousafzai

Malala is from Pakistan. She campaigns for education for all. She survived an attack by a gunman who was against girls going to school. She went on to become the youngest person to be awarded a Nobel Peace Prize.

Stop climate change

"It is still not too late to act. It will take a far-reaching vision, it will take courage." Greta, speaking at the European Parliament, 2019.

No matter how old you are, you can help to lead the way to a better world. Here are some young activists who have become known for speaking up for their causes and inspiring others to do the same.

Difference is wonderful

Schuyler Bailer

Schuyler was the first openly transgender swimmer in the National Collegiate Athletic Association (NCAA), Division I, the highest level of college sports. Being trans means feeling like you are a different gender from the one you were born with. In Schuyler's case, he was born with a female body but now lives as a male. He has won awards for his activism and sporting achievements.

Speaking up for kids

"I will speak out for the millions of children and young people whose voices have been silenced." Millie, 2018.

Millie Bobby Brown

As a high profile actor, Millie is determined to put her fame to good use. The youngest ever UNICEF goodwill ambassador, she aims to shine a light on the rights of children across the world.

Nikki Christou

Nikki was born with a rare medical condition called AVM (arteriovenous malformation), which affects how she looks. She started a vlog under the name Nikki Lilly to raise awareness of facial disfigurement and promote the acceptance of difference.

Little community library

Setting up a small free library creates community spirit. People can stop by to pick up a book, drop off ones they'd like to donate, and share their favorites with the community.

Share the love

A book can take you on a magical adventure or teach you a useful skill. Not everyone has books at home, but everyone can borrow from the library.

Vera Cruz

SMALL LIBRARY

Free

Little libraries don't have to look like school libraries. You can decorate them however you want.

Shake it off

People might take a book and not put one back. Try not to worry—not everyone will understand your library project, but you're doing something great.

Free books

Put a clear sign somewhere on your library so people know they are allowed to borrow the books.

Spark a change

Little libraries show that someone in the neighborhood is working to build a better community. It may even inspire people to make cool things themselves.

Put your library where people can easily find it. You want plenty of people to share the books.

You're in charge

People will enjoy using a well-cared-for library. Check for any leaks in the roof. If any books get damp and moldy, recycle them and replace with new, fresh reading material.

Get your voice heard

Crafting a great speech

To write a great speech, focus on two or three main points, grab attention with powerful facts, and use a style you're comfortable with when you're speaking aloud.

Throughout history, great speakers have inspired others to take action with stirring speeches. Public speaking can be a bit scary, especially at first. Here are a few useful tips.

Where can you make your voice heard?

Participating in a debate club or giving a presentation in class are good ways to practice public speaking.

Speaking with confidence

Practice in front of friends, or video yourself to see what works. Look up at your audience and speak clearly. Breathe deeply to calm any nerves.

You got this!

Great speakers from history

Nelson Mandela

Mandela's powerful speeches include one he made when he was sent to prison for his political views in 1964.

Eleanor Roosevelt

Roosevelt's brilliant speeches, such as 1948's The Struggle for Human Rights, helped to bring about the Universal Declaration of Human Rights.

Abraham Lincoln

Delivered in 1863, Lincoln's Gettysburg Address was aimed at unifying the country and providing direction for the future.

To make the world a better place, we must fight for equality for everyone. We have to make difficult choices about how we behave and what we do. In this chapter, you'll learn about these tough challenges and how we can all help to make our planet a better and fairer place for humanity.

Get information

Read books, follow the news, listen to podcasts, and consider things from different angles to get a fully rounded picture.

Use your talents

Activism can take lots of different forms. Try doing some things you enjoy, whether it's making music, designing banners, or writing poetry. Have fun!

Join forces

It's good to share thoughts and ideas with others. Find out if there's a local group you can join or team up with other people who share your passion.

How to be an

You don't need to launch a formal campaign to start getting your message out there. Voice your opinion and try to make an impact.

"I believe we are here on the planet Earth to live, grow up and do what we can to make this world a better place for all people to enjoy freedom." Rosa Parks, US civil rights activist (1913-2005).

activist

Are you someone who wants to campaign for ways to make the world a better place? Here's how to get started.

Finding your cause

There are so many good causes out there, it's difficult to know where to start! This quiz will help you find the issue closest to your heart.

1 What do you dream of being when you grow up?

A. A veterinarian
B. A teacher or doctor
C. An author or an artist
D. A scientist

2 What is your dream pet?

A. A horse
B. A dog
C. A cactus
D. I prefer animals to live in the wild

3 Which of these things would you be most willing to give up?

A. Eating meat and fish
B. Being driven to school
C. The latest cool sneakers
D. Flying on a plane to exciting vacation destinations

4 If you could get everyone to make only ONE change for a better world, what would it be?

A. Becoming vegetarian
B. Putting their garbage in the recycling
C. Helping homeless people and refugees
D. Stoping plastic use

5 If you could put one picture on your wall, what would it be?

A. A puppy
B. A picture of you and a friend
C. A sports hero
D. A photo of the Earth from space

6 If you could go back in time, which period would you visit?

A. The age of the dinosaurs
B. The time of the very first human beings
C. The period of the ancient Egyptians
D. The era of the moon landings

What is your dream vacation?

A. Seeing the wildlife in Serengeti National Park
B. Visiting a bustling city like New York or Singapore
C. Making friends somewhere new to you
D. Taking a sustainable tourism trip to the Great Barrier Reef

10

What's your favorite subject in school?

A. Science
B. Art
C. History
D. Social Studies

8

Which of these human rights is the most important to you?

A. The right to play
B. The right to express an opinion
C. The right to choose your friends
D. The right to healthy food and clean water

Mostly Ds

You understand the importance of protecting our planet and tackling climate change. You would make a great **environmental activist**.

Mostly Cs

You care deeply about big issues affecting humanity and would be a fabulous **human rights activist**.

7

If scientists could invent just ONE of these inventions, which one should it be?

A. Hologram pets so you could keep a tiger in your room
B. Teleportation so you could visit anyone you like in a split second
C. A backpack with infinite capacity to carry all your stuff
D. Hoverboards or broomsticks so you could fly

Mostly Bs

You're sociable, curious, and always finding ways to make the place you live better for everyone. You'd be an amazing **community activist**.

Mostly As

You're passionate about animals of all kinds, from anteaters to zebras, which means you'd make a fantastic **animal rights activist**.

Poster power

Well worded flyers, beautiful banners, and punchy posters can be powerful tools in getting your message across. Use these top tips to create your own unique campaign materials.

Stick to bold colors and use large text.

Test out eye-catching slogans or try a simple play on words. This poster plays on the term "Plan B," meaning a backup alternative.

THERE IS NO PLANET B

Banners

When there is a news story about a protest, it is often the banners that appear on the front pages of newspapers around the world.

Banner-making event!

Tuesday at 4 p.m.

Town Hall

Everyone welcome

Posters

A poster is designed to be hung up somewhere it will be seen. It is used to tell people about an issue or a planned event, so it's important to ensure all the relevant details are included there, such as the time and place of your event.

Don't forget to check your spelling and grammar. You don't want your message to be noticed for the wrong reason!

Flyers

Smaller than a poster, a flyer is often handed out or sent through the mail. Flyers take time to distribute, but they can help you reach large numbers of people.

Remember that the person reading the information might not know anything about the subject yet. Keep it simple.

PLAStic PROTESt

Park School gym June 1, 6 p.m.

If you care about our planet and you're worried about the plastic clogging up the oceans, join our protest to demand an end to single-use plastic.

Stand up for your rights

In 1989, an international agreement set out the rights of every child in the world, no matter who they are or where they are born.

The Rights of the Child

Not all children live in situations where their rights are secure. Their governments and families are responsible for protecting them.

You have the right to a safe place to live.

You have the right to food.

You have the right to go to school.

You have the right not to be hurt or mistreated.

You have the right to privacy.

Bring out your best

The Rights of the Child treaty includes a section encouraging children to develop their talents and abilities, respect others, and protect the environment.

I have the right to information.

I have the right to play!

I have the right to an opinion.

I have the right to have a name.

I have the right to choose my friends.

What is discrimination?

Discrimination is when someone is treated unfairly because of who they are. This might mean their race, religion, gender, gender identity, age, sexual orientation, disability, physical difference, or any other characteristic.

Spotting it

Discrimination can be obviously nasty behavior or a more subtle way of treating people differently.

Why does discrimination happen?

People discriminate against others, sometimes without realizing it, to put others down and make themselves feel better. It is a type of bullying.

What is

No one has the right to treat someone else badly or unfairly. Discrimination can take many forms, so it's important to

Less = more

A world without discrimination means less hatred and more happiness, less intolerance and more inclusivity, less unfairness and more equality!

Stereotypes

Stereotypes are broad, general ideas that a group of people are all the same. For example, "all teenagers are lazy."

Prejudice

A prejudice is a negative, fixed idea about someone that's not based on facts. An example of prejudice is thinking someone of a different race is inferior.

Lack of understanding

When people aren't encouraged to appreciate diversity, they might fear people who are different from themselves.

Assumptions

Without realizing it, people make assumptions based on stereotypes. They might not want to trust a teenager with something important if they think all teens are lazy.

Barriers

Some disabled people are prevented from participating equally. For example, a wheelchair user cannot use steps to access a building.

discrimination?

understand what it is. We have to do whatever we can to tackle it and make sure our society is equal for all.

Kendrick Lamar
US hip-hop artist Lamar is known for the hard-hitting political activism in his music. His 2015 track "Alright" became the unofficial anthem of the Black Lives Matter movement.

Joan Baez
Baez campaigns for social justice, peaceful protest, and civil rights. Her 1963 cover version of the stirring gospel song "We Shall Overcome" is a classic protest anthem.

Sonita Alizadeh
Afghan "raptivist" Alizadeh's music tackles the topic of forced marriage, which she herself fought to escape. She won international acclaim with her song "Brides for Sale" in 2014.

Turn it up!

In addition to expressing emotions, music has the power to reflect issues in society and spread a message. These are just some of the musical artists who have called for change throughout history.

Sam Cooke
Soul singer and activist Sam Cooke's 1964 song "A Change is Gonna Come" captured the struggle to end racial discrimination in 1960s America.

Lady Gaga
Gaga is known for using her fame to promote social issues, particularly equality, which is the subject of her thumping 2011 hit "Born This Way."

Nina Simone
A powerful singer who also cared about justice, Simone was actively involved in the 1960s civil rights movement in the US. She released the civil rights anthem "To Be Young, Gifted and Black" in 1970.

Bob Marley
Jamaican reggae singer Marley wrote songs about human rights. Songs such as his 1975 hit "Get Up, Stand Up" gave a voice to poor and oppressed people across the world.

My campaign

A campaign is a series of things you do to help your cause. A good campaign has to be planned out.

Get set...

Set a goal
Write down what you aim to achieve with your campaign.

Raise awareness

Get people to change their behavior

Get a change in the law or the rules

Raise money for charity

Research
Before you start your campaign, do as much research as you can.

Talk to lots of different people to get their views

Double-check your facts

Read news stories about your cause

Find out about what worked well on similar campaigns

Choose your methods
What is the best way to achieve your goals?

Put up posters and give out flyers

Get the local newspaper to cover the campaign

Ask your principal how you can achieve your goal at school

Start a petition

Go!

Change can take some time

Liftoff!
Starting a campaign is exciting, but don't be disheartened if things don't happen right away.

Learning from situations that don't go as planned is a key part of the process

Flying high
What is working well and what isn't? Remember, plans can change as you go along.

Success
Give yourself credit for everything you achieve. The sky is the limit!

Marley Dias
Frustrated that all her school books featured white, male characters, Marley Dias campaigned for 1,000 books with black, female main characters. She collected 9,000!

Save the porcupines!
Ahmet and Ismail wanted to stop porcupines from being run over. Their brightly colored signs helped reduce porcupine deaths by 60 percent.

WWF
WWF-Türkiye

Raising money

A great way to help a charity or cause is to raise funds for it. Whether it's providing aid after a natural disaster or buying equipment for a hospital, support for charities is always needed.

Spare change

You'll be surprised by how much you can save just by collecting coins in a jar or a piggy bank. Add any spare change you get when out shopping or set aside some of your allowance.

Halloween hijinks
Why not plan a themed event and sell tickets to it? Apple bobbing is always popular. Halloween is always popular.

Race against time
Take the challenge of a sponsored swim meet or fun run for charity.

Bake up a storm
Hold a bake sale with some friends. Who can bake and sell the tastiest cupcakes?

Resale value
If old toys or games are gathering dust, you can ask your parents to sell them online and donate the proceeds.

Smart donation
Charities can make money from recycling old phones and tablets, even broken ones.

Donate it
Donate things you don't need to thrift stores. They can sell the items to raise money.

At the car wash
Earn money by washing cars... bucket, soap, and sponge and you are ready to go!

Protests from the past

Take action

Actions often speak louder than words. It is useful to talk, but you also need to show what you believe in.

Emmeline Pankhurst

The Suffragettes broke laws as a type of protest. They damaged property and went on marches until women in Britain were given the right to vote. Some of them were sent to prison.

Start with yourself

Before you criticize other people, look at your own actions. It can be tough to make sacrifices for what you believe in, but it's worth it.

Mahatma Gandhi

Gandhi was a master of peaceful protests. In 1930, he went on a very long march across India that attracted worldwide attention. Gandhi eventually helped India to gain its independence from Britain.

You are the latest in a long line of amazing activists who have used the power of protest. Here are some smart things that famous figures of the past did to help bring about change.

Sports protests

Black Power salute

At the 1968 Olympics, African-American athletes Tommie Smith and John Carlos each raised a black-gloved fist to protest against racial injustice.

Dream big

When it comes to making a change, nothing is more important than imagination. Before you can make a real change, dream about how a better world could be.

Aboriginal flag

Cathy Freeman raised the Aboriginal flag during the Olympic games in 2000. This was to celebrate her indigenous Australian heritage.

Dr. Martin Luther King Jr.

Dr. King was a powerful speaker. He used the magic of words to help people see how the world would be better without racist laws and attitudes.

Taking the knee

In 2016, some football players, including Colin Kaepernick (center), went down on one knee during the national anthem to protest against racism and police violence.

65

Bring water and snacks and make sure you pack for the weather.

How to go on a protest march

One way to show people power is to join a protest march for your cause. Marches get an issue noticed, which helps to change laws and shape history.

Make a big, bold sign with your message.

Make some noise! Cheer for the speakers, blow a whistle, or start a chant.

Remember, you can join for only part of the march. Enjoy the atmosphere!

If you're feeling worried

Large crowds can be overwhelming. Being prepared will help you to stay calm and safe.

 Have a plan for what to do if you get separated.

Check the schedule and planned route before the march. This is often published on a website or in the local press.

 Carry contact numbers for everyone in your group.

Tell your group if you need to stop for a break.

Arrange exactly where you will meet at the start and end.

Spotting fake news

"Fake news" means stories that have been made up or exaggerated to influence people. It's trickier than ever to figure out which stories you can trust, since so much information is available. Here are a few common signs to look out for.

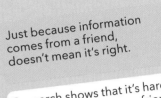

Chicken

Just because information comes from a friend, doesn't mean it's right.

Research shows that it's hard to spot fake news. Your friend might share some in error.

Or they may have picked a story that only tells one side of a complicated issue.

Ask yourself if the news source is well-known, reliable, and if the article was written by a reputable journalist. Does this website look like a good place to find news?

https://chickenoverlord.com/birdeatbird

Chicken opens new restaurant

Watch out for jokers

Some stories are written as joke news, either to make people laugh or to try to trick them. Some comedy "news" sites look a lot like real sites, and even journalists have believed fake news by mistake. Be aware!

THE NEWS NOW

Chicken lands on moon

Headlines can be misleading...

News stories often have shocking headlines designed to make people buy the publication or to boost the number of people visiting a website. Reading on, you might find that the story doesn't back up the headline or that you have to read through several pages to find anything relating to the headline at all.

... and so can pictures

Software can be used to alter images and show things that never happened. It's especially hard to tell if low-quality images on the Internet have been faked.

Try reading about the same event from a few different news sources to get a balanced picture.

"Fact-checking" means making sure a fact is true by consulting reliable sources, such as people who saw something happen. YouTubers aren't under pressure to fact-check—they can say anything! YouTube can be amazing, but remember to make up your own mind about things.

Okay guys, the Chicken is evil

♥ 69

Environment

Protecting the environment is vitally important for the future of our planet. This chapter explores how you can be part of making a better world for all life on Earth, from protecting animals to slowing down climate change.

How to be an environmental activist

If you're passionate about protecting our planet and you're looking to get involved in environmental activism, there are lots of ways to help.

Volunteer in your community

Check out kid-friendly activities going on in your area, such as tree-planting campaigns.

Eco-friendly life

Activism begins with the choices we make every day. Start by turning off the faucet while brushing your teeth.

"My dad taught me that we have a responsibility to protect the Earth the way our ancestors did. The world is seeing how powerful young people are." Xiuhtezcatl Martinez, US climate change activist, 2018.

Join a movement

Consider joining a national or international organization to keep up to date with news and campaigns.

Don't be defeated!

Remember that every single step you take to help matters.

Animal activism

Because they can't speak up for themselves, animals need us to use our voices for them. We can help protect animals by making good choices.

Animal testing

Make sure that the products you buy are cruelty-free. Testing beauty products on animals is illegal in many countries, but not everywhere.

Respect wildlife

Enjoy getting out into nature, but make sure not to disrupt any creatures living there, including when you are on vacation.

Wild garden

You can create a sanctuary for wildlife no matter how small your space. Plant a mix of flowers and plants that will attract birds, butterflies, and bees.

Protect habitats

Oil palms, which produce palm oil, are grown on huge plantations. Rain forest is cleared to make room for them, leaving orangutans with nowhere to live. Try to choose products that do not contain palm oil.

Be the best pet owner

Before getting a pet, it's important to research everything they will need. You need to be sure you can give your pet a happy, healthy life.

Eat organic

Animals farmed organically have more space, natural food, and higher standards of welfare. Choose organic meat and eggs where possible.

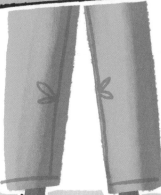

A meaty problem

A huge number of animals are raised for food. This is damaging the environment and contributing to climate change. Swapping meat for vegetables is a big way to make a difference, whether it's going vegetarian on some days or giving up animal products altogether.

Fart!

Cows create **65 percent** of the greenhouse gases that come from farming.

Buuurrp!

Most methane from cows comes from burps. More than a billion cow burps happen every 90 seconds!

Too many cows

Cows provide us with beef, milk, cheese, and materials such as leather. Their dung can even be used as garden fertilizer. There is such high demand for these things that huge areas of rain forest have been cleared to raise cattle.

Food energy

Farming animals for food uses much more energy and water than growing vegetables or grains. Meat production uses a lot of land, but provides only 18 percent of the energy people get from food. Non-meat foods usually do less damage to the environment.

17% of farmland is used to grow vegetables and grains

83% of farmland is used to produce meat

Nuts

Growing nuts creates only 1 percent of the greenhouse gases as the same amount of beef.

Fish

Farming fish, such as salmon, creates only 17 percent of beef's greenhouse gases.

Lentils

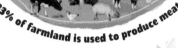

Lentils have a similar impact as nuts and are a protein-packed alternative to meat.

Eat the rainbow

Did you know that different-colored plants provide us with different vitamins? Try eating as many colors as you can!

Veganism

Vegans do not eat food that comes from animals, including meat, milk, and eggs.

Green living

More than half of the world's population now lives in cities, and that number is growing. Whether you live in a city, a smaller town, or somewhere more rural, it is essential to make sure that where you live is as eco-friendly and healthy as it can be.

From the top down

A "green roof" that's covered in plants improves air quality and is a haven for wildlife.

Solar panels provide renewable, pollution-free energy for homes.

Some tall buildings house bees on the roof!

Birdhouses and feeders help birds to survive. Their songs bring nature into a city.

Well-designed green buildings and neighborhoods are proven to make people happier.

Home, sweet home

Green buildings have lots of natural light. They are also energy-efficient, staying cool in summer and warm in winter.

Flower and herb boxes brighten up gray urban streets.

Trees produce oxygen, absorb pollution, shelter wildlife, and look beautiful.

Energy-saving streetlights switch on only when someone is passing.

Restricting the use of polluting vehicles makes the air cleaner. Breathing in good quality air is great for our health.

LOW EMISSION ZONE

Clean air makes it much nicer to get outside for some healthy exercise.

Getting around

Providing safe cycling lanes means more people will choose to travel by bike.

Pet owners are more likely to talk to their neighbors. Chatting to other people builds a community.

climate change

The temperature of our beautiful planet is rising to dangerous levels. We know that human activity is causing this. So, what can we do?

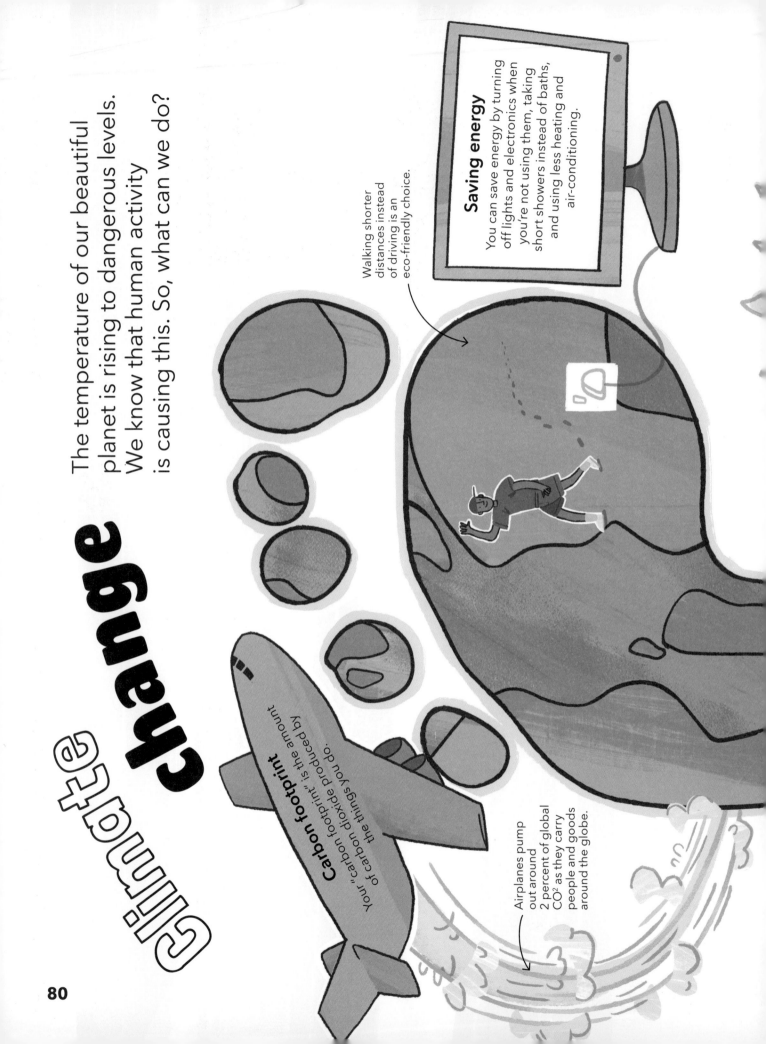

Carbon footprint
A "carbon footprint" is the amount of carbon dioxide produced by the things you do.

Airplanes pump out around 2 percent of global CO_2 as they carry people and goods around the globe.

Walking shorter distances instead of driving is an eco-friendly choice.

Saving energy
You can save energy by turning off lights and electronics when you're not using them, taking short showers instead of baths, and using less heating and air-conditioning.

What is global warming?

Burning fossil fuels increases carbon dioxide and other greenhouse gases in our atmosphere. These gases trap the sun's heat. More gases mean that the atmosphere warms up, creating global warming.

Grow it yourself

A good way to ensure your food doesn't have to travel far is to grow your own. You don't need much space for a small fruit or vegetable patch.

Foods grown in your home country have the lowest carbon footprint.

Reduce, reuse, recycle

Constantly buying new things and discarding the old ones takes a big toll on the environment. Reducing the amount we buy and throw away helps to save huge amounts of energy.

Repair torn clothes rather than throwing them away.

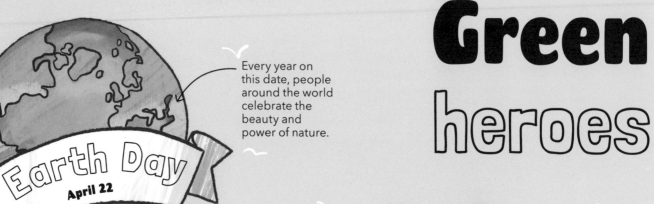

Green heroes

Every year on this date, people around the world celebrate the beauty and power of nature.

Earth Day
April 22

Preserve nature

"The more clearly we can focus our attention on the wonders and realities of the universe about us, the less taste we shall have for destruction."

Rachel Carson

Marine biologist Carson's 1962 book *Silent Spring* showed the dangers of chemical pesticides, sparking the formation of the US Environmental Protection Agency.

Celebrate our planet

"The natural world is the greatest source of excitement. It is the source of so much that makes life worth living."

Sir David Attenborough

Through his incredible TV shows, such as *Blue Planet*, Attenborough has inspired millions of people to take better care of nature.

Environmental activists raise awareness of the importance of protecting our planet. Just one person can make a big difference!

Defending the land

Chico Mendez

Chico Mendez was a brave community organizer. He led a group of rubber plantation workers who joined together to protect the Brazilian rain forest from deforestation.

Start a change

"You cannot protect the environment unless you empower people. You [must] help them understand that these resources are their own."

Vandana Shiva

This scientist set up a program that promotes organic farming and planting a wide range of crops, which is better for the soil than planting just one type of crop.

Julia Butterfly Hill

To stop a logging company from cutting down trees in California, Hill lived in a 1,500-year-old redwood tree for more than two years.

Wangari Maathai

Maathai founded the Green Belt Movement, a campaign that helps Kenyan women to improve their lives by planting trees. They have planted more than 51 million so far!

So, what's the problem?

Our oceans have become a dumping ground for the plastic we throw away. Plastic pollutes the water and harms sea creatures if they eat it.

Research what products are made of before you buy.

Use paper or reusable stainless steel straws instead of plastic ones.

The plastic problem

For more than 100 years, we have used plastic for everything from packing food to making furniture. Plastic stays in the environment for a very long time, so all this waste has created a big problem.

Inspiring sisters

The Bye Bye Plastic Bags campaign was set up by schoolgirls Melati and Isabel Wijsen from Bali, Indonesia. It led to single-use plastics being banned in Bali.

Choose products that aren't packaged in plastic.

What can we do?

The choices we make every day can make a big difference. Try choosing plastic-free products and recycle as much as possible. One person can't solve the problem alone, but together we can do it!

Don't buy plastic bags, bottles, and utensils.

Animals are threatened by hunting, pollution, and habitat loss.

Conservation success stories

Human activity has changed the face of the planet, leaving less space for wildlife. Conservationists are people who help protect animals and their habitats. They have helped some species come back from the brink of extinction.

Giant panda
A crackdown on poaching (illegal hunting) and the creation of panda preserves in China have helped save the giant panda from extinction.

Tamarin
Since conservation efforts began in the 1980s, golden lion tamarin numbers have increased from just 200 to more than 1,000.

Save the whales

A campaign by members of the public led to a **ban** on whale hunting. The ban was introduced in most countries in 1986.

Kestrel
The Mauritius kestrel lives only on the island of Mauritius, which is in the Indian Ocean. It became one of the Earth's rarest birds, but the species has now bounced back.

Parakeet
The echo parakeet also lives only on Mauritius. At one point, only 10-12 birds remained. Now there are over 500.

Humpback whale
Known for their complex songs, humpback whales were once nearly wiped out, with only 10,000 animals remaining. There are now 80,000.

How are people helping?

Park rangers
Rangers working in nature preserves risk their lives to protect endangered species from poachers who want to sell illegal animal products, such as ivory.

Tortoise
Nearly 2,000 rare giant Galápagos tortoises have been bred and released back into the wild.

Indigenous people
People with a strong connection to their land, such as the Sami reindeer herders of Lapland, help protect animal life. The Sami oppose mining that threatens important grazing land.

As you start on your journey to making the world a better place, don't be afraid to fail. The important thing is to keep striving to make a difference. You are part of a generation with the power to change things. Your voice counts and the future is yours to shape.

Find out more

How can you get involved? Here's a list of organizations, websites, and campaigns to give you more information and ideas.

Childnet
Provides advice and information about how children can stay safe online.

Cosmic Kids
Teaches children how to remain calm and relaxed using yoga and mindfulness videos.

Do Something! Foodwise
A campaign that teaches people about how the food they eat affects the environment and gives tips on how they can reduce food waste.

The Fairtrade Foundation
An organization that works to make sure that the farmers and workers who produce our food get paid fairly.

Freecycle
Encourages people to give away items they no longer need but that are too good to throw away. This way, less waste ends up in landfills.

Friends of the Earth
A group of charities from all over the world that works together to defend the environment and educate people about important environmental issues.

Greenpeace
An organization that works to make the world a greener and more peaceful place.

Keep America Beautiful
A nonprofit organization that encourages communities to take action to improve their public spaces.

Kids Against Bullying
A website that allows kids to share experiences about bullying and learn about the topic in an interesting and interactive way.

Kidscape
Provides children and adults with advice about how to deal with and prevent bullying.

March for Our Lives
Student-led movement that campaigns for stronger gun control laws in the United States.

Mental Health America

Supports people with mental health problems. It campaigns to improve services on a national and local level and promote greater understanding.

National Alliance on Mental Illness

An organization that works to raise awareness of mental illness and helps people affected to understand how they are feeling and find support.

Nourish Interactive

A website with games, tools, and tips on how to live and eat healthily.

Rescuing Leftover Cuisine

A food waste prevention organization that takes leftover food from businesses and distributes it to communities and people in need.

Save the Children

An organization that works toward making the world a better and safer place for children. It focuses on ensuring that kids have an education and health care.

School Strike for Climate

A movement of students, started by Greta Thunberg, that protests for action on climate change by refusing to go to school.

Sierra Club

An environmental organization that works to protect wild places and public land in the US from deforestation and pollution.

Unicef

Provides vulnerable children around the world with the education, health care, and protection they need and deserve.

United We Dream

An immigrant youth-led community that creates welcoming spaces for all young people.

Vegetarian Society

Inspires, educates, and supports people on how to be vegetarian. Provides a range of vegetarian recipes and advice to those who are newly vegetarian.

Wellness in the Schools

A nonprofit organization that works with schools to teach kids healthy habits that promote wellness.

World Wildlife Fund

A charity that works to protect animals and their homes from pollution, deforestation, and danger, such as poaching.

YoungMinds

An organization that fights to make sure that children and young people with mental health problems are cared for and supported.

Zero Hour

Youth-led organization that takes action to fight climate change.

Glossary

activism
Speaking out or acting on something you do not agree with in order for it to change

ancestor
Person from whom someone is descended

ban
To stop people from being allowed to do something

bullying
Behavior intended to hurt someone physically or emotionally. It may be aimed at a person due to their race, religion, background, disability, or other difference

campaign
Carrying out a series of actions in order to achieve a goal

charity
Organization that collects money and uses it to help people

climate change
Change in temperature and weather across the Earth that can be natural or caused by human activity

conservation
Protecting environments and plant and animal life

culture
Beliefs and way of life of a group of people, including their art, clothes, music, and food

deforestation
Cutting down trees and destroying forests

discrimination
Treating a group of people unfairly because of their characteristics or beliefs, for example, their race or religion

donate
To give something, usually money

eco-friendly
Something that does not harm the environment

equality
Same rights for everyone

endangered
Rare animal or plant that could soon become extinct

energy-efficient
Something that only uses the amount of energy needed, without waste

environment
Area in which plants, animals, and people live

extinction
When a species or type of animal or plant dies out completely

fossil fuels
Fuels made from animals or plants that died millions of years ago—for example, coal. There are limited amounts of fossil fuels, and burning them harms the environment

global warming
When average temperatures rise all around the world

greenhouse gases
Gases in the Earth's atmosphere that trap heat and warm the planet

human right
Right that every person has

justice
Fair behavior or treatment

mindfulness
Being aware of yourself in body and mind

movement
Group of people who work together to change something and share their ideas

organization
Group of people who work to achieve a common goal

petition
Document that lots of people can sign; it asks an authority to do something about a particular cause

pollution
Something that harms the environment, for example, by getting into the air, water, or soil

prejudice
Having unfair, usually bad, opinions about people without good reason

preserve
Area that protects wild animals from hunters or that limits hunting by law

protest
Showing that you disagree with something by speaking out or fighting for it to change

race
Group of people who originate in the same part of the world and share physical characteristics

racism
Behaving negatively toward other people because of their race

recycle
To use something again or to make it into something new

rights
Freedoms that people are guaranteed by law, for example, the right to freedom of speech

single-use plastic
Plastic that can only be used once before having to be thrown away

species
Group of plants or animals that share similar features

stereotype
Broad, general idea that a group of people are all the same. For example, "all teenagers are lazy"

strike
When people protest by refusing to do something

tradition
Something that has been done in the same way for a long time

Index

Acknowledgments

The author would like to thank First News and Nicky Cox MBE for their support. **DK** would like to thank the following: Lizzie Davey and Abigail Luscombe for additional editorial help, Jaileen Kaur for coordinating the hi-res images, Polly Goodman for proofreading, Helen Peters for the index, and Tony Stevens of Disability Rights UK and Sherese Jackson for their comments on the book.

Quote attribution and references:
pp34-35 Greta Thunberg: "You are never too small to make a difference." Speaking at COP24 December 2019. **pp40-41** Millie Bobby Brown:"I will speak out for millions of children and young people…" Speaking at a press conference on being announced as UNICEF's youngest-ever goodwill ambassador on World Children's day, November 2018. **pp48-49** Rosa Parks: "I believe we are here on planet Earth to…" From Life Magazine, "The Meaning of Life" feature, December 1988. **p61** "Save the porcupines!" text written using information from the WWF. **pp72-73** Xiuhtezcatl Martinez: "My dad taught me…" From his interview with The Guardian, May 2018. **pp82-83** Rachel Carson: "The more clearly we can focus our attention on the wonders and realities…" From her book, Silent Spring, 1962. Sir David Attenborough: "The natural world is the greatest source of excitement…" From the BBC website. Wangari Maathai: "You cannot protect the environment unless you empower people…" Said on her website "The Green Belt movement".

The publisher would like to thank the following for their kind permission to reproduce their photographs:

(Key: a-above; b-below/bottom; c-center; f-far; l-left; r-right; t-top)

6-7 naturepl.com: Guy Edwardes (Background). **8-9 Depositphotos Inc:** Artkamalov (Background). **12 Dreamstime.com:** Katarzyna Bialasiewicz (c). **13 Dorling Kindersley:** Pedal Pedlar (ca). **14-15 Dreamstime.com:** Tommason. **15 Dorling Kindersley:** The Real Aeroplane Company (tr). **22 Dorling Kindersley:** Steve Lyne (br). **Fotolia:** Eric Isselee (bl). **23 Alamy Stock Photo:** FogStock (tr). **Dorling Kindersley:** ha London (tl). **Rex by Shutterstock:** Todd Williamson / January Images / Shutterstock (clb). **24-25 123RF.com:** Vassiliy Prikhodko (Background). **26-27 Depositphotos Inc:** Artkamalov (Background). **28 Dreamstime.com:** Monkey Business Images (bc); Pressmaster (clb). **29 Alamy Stock Photo:** BSIP SA (c). **32-33 Dreamstime.com:** Dmitry Zimin (c). **32 Alamy Stock Photo:** Age Fotostock (cla); Asia (tl). **33 Alamy Stock Photo:** Age Fotostock (br). **Dorling Kindersley:** Frome & District Agricultural Society (tr); National Music Museum (cla). **Dreamstime.com:** Jill Battaglia (tc). **34 Alamy Stock Photo:** JG Photography (ca); MediaPunch Inc (clb). **Getty Images:** Joe Raedle / Staff (tr). **35 Alamy Stock Photo:** Daniel Bockwoldt / DPA (ca). **Getty Images:** NurPhoto (crb). **36 Alamy Stock Photo:** ZUMA Press Inc. (cb). **Dreamstime.com:** Deyangeorgiev (cla); Anthony Aneese Totah Jr (br); Igor Zakharevich (bc, bl). **37 Alamy Stock Photo:** Jeffrey Isaac Greenberg 3 (c); Paramvir Singh (Background). **40 Getty Images:** John van Hasselt - Corbis (br); Fairfax Media (bl). **41 Getty Images:** Emma McIntyre / KCA2018 (bl); The Washington Post (cr). **Rex by Shutterstock:** Ken McKay / ITV / Shutterstock (br). **42 Alamy Stock Photo:** David Litschel (cr); Rosanne Tackaberry / Little Free Library® is a registered trademark of Little Free Library, LTD, a 501(c)(3) nonprofit organization. (cr); Mark Summerfield (crb). **43 Alamy Stock Photo:** Felix Choo / Little Free Library® is a registered trademark of Little Free Library, LTD, a 501(c)(3) nonprofit organization. (bl); Mark Summerfield (cla); Jim West (tr); Philip Game (cr).

45 Alamy Stock Photo: RGB Ventures / SuperStock (br). **Getty Images:** Georges De Keerle (cr); Francis Miller / The LIFE Picture Collection (crb). **46-47 Depositphotos Inc:** Artkamalov (Background). **53 Dreamstime. com:** Betelgejze (t); Marish (b). **55 Dreamstime.com:** Elnur (c); Wavebreakmedia Ltd. (bl). **56-57 Dreamstime.com:** Mishoo (Background). **58 Alamy Stock Photo:** ZUMA Press, Inc. (ca). **Getty Images:** Joe Raedle (cla); Randy Shropshire / WireImage (tr). **59 Alamy Stock Photo:** Archive PL (ca). **Getty Images:** Lynn Goldsmith / Corbis Premium Historical (crb); Hulton Archive / Archive Photos (cl); Marina Bay Sands (cra). **61 Alamy Stock Photo:** WENN Rights Ltd (cra). **Dreamstime. com:** Scol22 (tr, br/Frame). **WWF-Turkey:** Esra Turam, Education Programme Manager (br). **64 Getty Images:** Bettmann (bl); Rühe / ullstein bild (bc). **65 Alamy Stock Photo:** The History Collection (cra). **Getty Images:** Mike Powell (cr); Steve Schapiro (bl); San Jose Mercury News (br). **66-67 Getty Images:** Saeed Khan / AFP (t). **68 Dreamstime. com:** Alexlmx (tr); Paul Hakimata / Phakimata (bc); Vladimirs Prusakovs (bc/Chicken). **Fotolia:** Anatoliy Babiy / bloomua (b). **69 Dreamstime.com:** Axstokes (br); Vladimirs Prusakovs (c/Chicken., br/Chicken); Natthawut Nungensanthia (clb/Chicken). **NASA:** (clb); NASA / JPL-Caltech / Space Science Institute (c). **70-71 Depositphotos Inc:** Artkamalov (Background). **72-73 NASA:** MSFC / Bill Cooke (Background); Ocean Biology Processing Group at NASA's Goddard Space Flight Center (bc). **74 123RF.com:** peterwaters (clb/Bee). **Dreamstime.com:** Alle (clb); Nilanjan Bhattacharya (br). **Getty Images:** Stockbyte / John Foxx (cla). **75 123RF. com:** Sergey Mironov / supernam (br). **Dreamstime.com:** Eric Isselee (cla); Theo Malings (cra); Photka (bc). **76 Alamy Stock Photo:** Jon Ongkiehong (c). **77 Alamy Stock Photo:** Jon Ongkiehong (c). **Dorling Kindersley:** Geoff Dann / Cotswold Farm Park, Gloucestershire (t/cow and calf). **Dreamstime.com:** Mike_kiev (t/cow); Supertrooper (t). **78 Dorling Kindersley:** Natural History Museum, London (ca/Box). **Dreamstime.com:** EmeraldUmbrellaStudio (ca); Mikael Damkier / Mikdam (cla). **78-79 Alamy Stock Photo:** Kim Petersen (t). **82 Alamy Stock Photo:** Jeff Gilbert (br). **Getty Images:** CBS (bl). **83 Getty Images:** AFP Contributor (bl); Antonio Scorza (cra); Amanda Edwards (crb); Andrew Lichtenstein / Sygma (br). **84 123RF.com:** Tatiana Popova / violin (cb/car); Aleksey Poprugin (crb, cb). **85 123RF.com:** Aleksey Poprugin (clb, cb). **Bye Bye Plastic Bags:** Andrew Wyton / Zissou / Karen Hoogland (tr). **Dreamstime.com:** Indigolotos (cb/bottle); Alfio Scisetti / Scisettialfio (crb); Penchan Pumila / Gamjai (cl, bl). **86-87 Dreamstime.com:** Paul Wolf / Paulwolf (c). **86 Dorling Kindersley:** Andrew Beckett (Illustration Ltd) (br). **Fotolia:** Eric Isselee (crb). **87 123RF.com:** Smileus (clb). **Alamy Stock Photo:** Nature Picture Library (tr); Xinhua (crb). **Dreamstime.com:** Erix2005 (bc). **naturepl.com:** Mark Carwardine (cra). **88-89 naturepl. com:** Wild Wonders of Europe / Bartocha (Background). **89 Dorling Kindersley:** Pedal Pedlar (bc). **92-93 Depositphotos Inc:** Artkamalov (Background). **94-95 Depositphotos Inc:** Artkamalov (Background). **96 Depositphotos Inc:** Artkamalov (Background)

All other images © Dorling Kindersley
For further information see: www.dkimages.com